www.crowepress.com
www.martamoranbishop.com

To the memory of my grandmother, Helen Springer Moran. Some of her verses written to entertain her three children inspired me to write Wee Three. You can find them within these pages. Most of them I expanded, a few were left as they were.

To my mother, Patricia Moran, who spent her life writing, reading, and correcting my English, my uncle, Al (Dink), who was my father figure and friend, and my aunt Pam, who remains my dear, sister-friend.

To my husband, Ken, who is my greatest cheerleader and friend, whose continual love and support allows me the time and energy to write.

Hazel Mitchell, thank you for your extraordinary illustrations, which so clearly depict my prose.

WEE THREE
A Mother's Love in Verse

Marta Moran Bishop
&
Helen Springer Moran

Illustrations:

Hazel Mitchell

UPSIDE-DOWN LAND

When tired of games and pictures too
And all my books I've read
And I can't think what else to do
I stand upon my head

Then I pretend in some strange lands
Across a fairy sea
The people all walk on their hands
Not right side up, like me

And then I wonder how they'd sleep
Upside down upon their beds
And how they'd ever, ever keep
Their hats upon their heads

I wonder too, if in these lands
The folks upon the street
Would wear their shoes upon their hands
Their gloves upon their feet

But mother says if they appeared
And met me on the street
They'd laugh, she's sure, and think me weird
For walking on my feet.

MOTHER'S FLOWER GARDEN

There's one kind she calls fox glove
But there are no foxes there
There are lady slippers that
A lady couldn't wear.

And Canterbury bells of blue
That never, never ring
And little johnnie-jump-ups
That don't jump or do a thing.

The trumpets on the trumpet vine
Are not a bit of use
But honeysuckle we can suck
And get the honey juice.

RESTLESS

I think I'll make an airplane, no
I think I'll make a kite
If I had all the things to make
A radio—I might.

Perhaps I'll use this piece of wood
To make myself a boat
A sail boat, no—a ferry boat
Or just a raft to float.

I really can't think what to make
On such a messy day
I wish the rain would finally stop
So I could go out to play.

Marta Moran Bishop

WISHING

Today I saw a bumblebee
A bumblebee or two
I thought I'd follow one and see
Where he was going to

He tasted first some lilacs tall
Buzzed among the clover
Went flying to the garden wall
Just went sailing over

I wish I were a bumblebee
And I know just what for
I'd fly into the cherry tree
Across the wall next door

I'd eat and eat while I was there
And never wash my face
Nor brush my teeth or comb my hair
But fly from place to place.

PRETENDING

I'm playing I'm a little mouse
I'm hiding everywhere

They mustn't ever see me
They mustn't know I'm there.

They wonder how the cracker crumbs
Got down behind the chair

They'll think t'was Pam that did it
And never know a mouse was there.

MY LITTLE GARDEN

Some little seeds so small and round
I planted nicely in the ground
All neatly in a little row
And then I watched for them to grow

And after many days had passed
I found that they had grown at last
And every single tiny one
Was popping up to see the sun.

SUMMER RAIN

It rained and rained and rained some more
We could not go outside the door

It pounded on the window pane
And poured like rivers down the drains

And then so very suddenly
The sun came out and laughed with glee

And there above us, oh so high
A rainbow stretched across the sky.

CINDERELLA MOTHER

When Mother's all dressed up to go
Out to a party or to a show
Before she leaves for house or town
We see her in her evening gown

Her evening gowns are long and low
And swish, as she walks to and fro
She's so beautiful to see
We think she really cannot be.

Our Ma, who 'tends us when we're sick
And helps us with our 'rithmetic
But when she's tucked us all in tight
Has kissed us and put out the light.

We're happy—for though she may look
Just like a princess in a book
Or Cinderella at the ball
She's our dear mother, after all.

FISHING

I went a-fishing in a brook
I had a worm, I had a hook
I had a pole, I had a line
I saw a fish that would be mine.

I sat, so very quietly
And waited, oh so patiently
'Though, all the day I wished my wish
I did not catch a single fish.

VACATIONS

We like to go 'most anywhere
And have such fun while we are there
But when it's time to leave, why then
We like to go back home again.

TRAVELING

Clackety, clackety, clackety clack
The wheels go over the railroad track
Taking us further and farther away
We're seeing the world in a single day

Rivers and forests and cities go by
While faster and faster and faster we fly
Oh, but its fun to go traveling far
And having our lunch in a dining car.

BIRD TRACKS UPON THE SNOW

Some tiny tracks are on the snow
A little bird was there, I know
A little bird that hopped

I looked to see where they would go
Those cunning bird tracks on the snow
When suddenly they stopped

Soon, I saw it so plain as day
He'd spread his wings and flown away
That was why they had stopped

I looked way up into the sky
And there I saw him flying high
My little bird that hopped.

LONELY

A small brown ant came running by
With antenna and a shiny eye
It looked as if he had a sack
Large green leaf upon his back

I asked him where he was going to
And what it was he had to do
All aquiver in his haste
He ran on by, no time to waste

A little toad came hopping by
He stopped to eat a butterfly
Soft and warm he did seem
Looking at me with eyes a gleam

He would not say a word to me
'Though I was nice as I could be
For when I said "hello" why then
He just went hopping off again.

SNOW MAGIC

Our garden is a fairyland, lovely to see
Off in the corner stands a white, frosted tree

The sugar plum bushes are all in a row
Their branches all a sparkle covered in snow

The ugly brown fence is quite hidden from sight
The bird house is wearing a bonnet of white

The feeders are covered with birds all a glow
They flock in for breakfast and dinner to go

Woodpeckers, Cardinals, and Blue Jays galore
A rainbow of colors they fly by our door.

CRICKET SONG

I love to hear the crickets
A-singing in the grass
I'd like to catch a cricket
And keep him in a glass

So then, when wintertime is here
And warmer days are gone
I'll have my little cricket near
To sing a summer's song.

TWO-GUN DINK

Better be careful and better watch out
For "Two-Gun Dink" is here about
We think its "Two-Gun," but who really knows
With a red bandana over his nose

With two guns, it's plain to see
He's a bandit, fierce as fierce can be
We're awfully scared and we'd like to run
For who's not afraid of the fierce, "Two-Gun?"

But what was there, he did not see
He stumbled over the root of a tree
So he isn't "Two-Gun" anymore
He's a little boy and his knee is sore.

HOSPITAL

We are in the hospital with the flu
No place for us to play, not much to do
Chasing each other 'round the room we sprayed
Water guns out of syringes we made

Racing up and down the halls we would zoom
Smiles and laughter banished the gloom
Soon it'll be back to bed for one and all
For making noise playing in the hall

We think they will send us all home real soon
If we don't stop acting like buffoons
"It is a hospital," we heard them say
Not a room for all of us to play.

MUMPS

Pam and Pat have got the mumps
Their necks are full of awful lumps

And they don't feel so very good
It hurts to eat; I wish they could

Our mother says 'most any day
Those horrid lumps will go away

But what I really want to know
Is where those horrid lumps do go?

THINKING

I am sick and I'm in bed
I have an ache inside my head
And funny bumps all over me

That are as itchy as can be
I have the chicken pox they say
And I've been thinking all the day

"Where did they come from?" I do pray
I wish they would go away today
I do say, "It is the dickens,"
I've not been near any chickens.

CLIMBING

When I climb up in a tree
As high as I can go
And look away down under me
The ground is far below

But I'm surprised because the sky
Looks just the same I've found
And is above me just as high
As when I'm on the ground.

THE WAY I GROW

It's very odd the way I grow
Sometimes it's fast, sometimes slow
Sometimes I seem to be quite small
And then again, I'm not at all

I'm little when I want to go
To see a moving picture show
And should I want to stay up late
I'm small and bedtime's always eight

I'm much too small to wear high heels
Or sit with grown-up folks at meals
And lots of other nice things too
I find that I'm too small to do

But if I've dirtied up my dress
When company's come, and I'm a mess
Or cry when soap gets in my eyes
Why, suddenly, I'm quite a size

And then they say that I'm too big
To get as dirty as a pig
And I'm too big they say, for shame
To cry about a little pain

I'm big when it is being brave
I'm big, they say, and must behave
But when it's anything at all

That's fun, I'm always much too small.

WONDERING

When we are young we cannot know
What it is like to bigger grow
But why do grown-ups, great and tall
So soon forget they once were small?

AT THE ZOO

When Pat and I went to the zoo
We saw a mother kangaroo
She had a pocket in her skin
To tuck her little babies in.

WHERE IS DINK?

Oh where is little Dink today?
We hope he hasn't gone away
Last night they tucked him safe in bed
And now a lump is there instead

But what a funny, wiggly lump
And when we tickle, see it jump!
We peeked and then what do you think
We found the lump was little Dink.

BABY BROTHER

He's very small and rather red
And has no hair upon his head
All he does is lie in bed
I wish we had a dog instead.

WHEN I'M A LADY

When I'm a lady I shall use
A nice red lipstick and some rouge
I'd like to have some now you know
But mother says that I must grow
To be a lady strong and tall
Or, I can't use lipstick at all

There's pretty Belle across the street
She wears high heels upon her feet
And has a lipstick and a beau
What did she do to make her grow?
She once was just as small as me
And now she's big, as big can be!

To grow like Belle across the street
I'll gladly eat my beans and meat
I'll nicely drink my milk all down
And wear a grin and not a frown
So then, perhaps, I'll quicker grow
And have a lipstick and a beau.

But I get, Oh! So sad and blue
No matter what I eat or do
For when I stand against the door
To see if I have grown some more
The same small size I seem to stay
I haven't grown since yesterday.

WHEN COMPANY COMES

We comb our hair and shine our shoes
And watch the manners that we use
We would not shame our mom or dad
By doing anything that's bad

At table we are so polite
We hold our forks and spoons just right
And always say, "thank you" and "please"
And "scuse me," if we cough or sneeze

But after they have gone, why then
We can just be ourselves again
And we are glad as we can be
That we don't have much company.

PAT

My mother always calls me "Pat,"
Except when I am bad
And then she says, "Patricia"
Sometimes she says it sad

Sometimes she says it not so kind
But when she says it very mad
It's then I know I'd better mind
Or else, I'll wish I had.

MR. CLANCY

I have a little turtle
Mr. Clancy is his name
He's very, very little
And he's very, very tame

I think he really likes me too
Although, he doesn't say
But if he does why is it that
He always runs away?

PUNISHED

I didn't put my rubbers on
And now my feet are wet
I know I should have done it
But I always do forget

So now I'm being punished
I can't go out to play
I hope that I'll remember, 'cause
I'm old enough they say.

A PONY

I'd like to have a pony
That I could ride
I'd spend the day upon it
I wouldn't leave its side

I'd sleep with it, in its stall
And curl up, all warm beside
If only I could have a pony
That I could ride.

BLOWING BUBBLES

We blow and blow and never stop
Until they're big enough to pop

And then we turn the pipe around
And blow them with a gurgling sound.

EATING

Potato is easy and so is rice
And spinach goes on a fork real nice

With beans and beets and carrots too
Just stick in the fork is all you do

But when its peas there is just one way
You have to push, or they roll away.

PUZZLED

I wonder why my little cat
Holds her tail up straight like that
While grown-up cats, I mostly find
Trail their tails along behind.

GRASSHOPPERS

Grasshoppers big, grasshoppers small
Hopping about in the grasses tall
There must be a million and maybe more
But all I can count is up to four.

BUSY

I'm busy, busy as can be
Making pies for Pat and me

Chocolate pies of mud I make
Then lay them in the sun to bake

I don't know why they can't see
When I'm as busy as can be

That I don't care if I'm a mess
I haven't time to wash and dress.

THE GOOD GROWN-UPS

When grown-up folk go down the street
They walk so proper on their feet
They never skip or hop or run
Or do the things we think are fun.

And when they talk, it's always low
Why we must shout, they do not know
Or why we fidget in our chairs
While they sit firmly down in theirs.

We wish they'd somehow understand
The world is wide and much too grand
With many places for us to go
And much to do before we grow.

THE CRYING CHAIR

Pam used to cry and cry and cry
And no one ever knew just why
So, there was not a thing to do
But let her cry 'til she was through

One day our mother said to her
"All right, Miss Pam, if you prefer
To cry so much you sit right there
And cry upon the crying chair."

Now Pam has stopped her crying spells
She seldom cries and never yells
And since she's never sitting there
They've put away the crying chair.

OUR HIDEAWAY

In our house is a small closet
Where we sit and keep our tasset
A slanted roof a place to play
On a snowy or rainy day

It is a treasure I can say
Where we can hide and play all day
Wonder Woman and Batman too
Princess or knight in castle blue

It is our bat cave dark as night
Batman and Robin find their might
In a castle upon a hill
Where princess and knight find their will

With tablecloths and napkins too
We have our raiment capes so blue
Wonder Woman, Superman too
We play before we bid adieu

Gossamer threads and jewelry bright
Pirates and maidens share their plight
In our so secret hideaway
We all pretend is on the bay

Hardened thieves, criminals we haul
Are locked in jail cells one and all
Napkins, tablecloths now become
Blankets and walls for all the scum

Fierce lawmen we all are today
Tomorrow pirates we may play
In our so secret hideaway
On a rainy or snowy day.

TIMOTHY TOMPKINS

Timothy Tompkins lived and ate
In a clean and roomy packing crate
T'was painted green and fine to see
Beneath a shady lilac tree

Above the door there hung a sign
"Timothy Tompkins—this is mine!"
So, common cats of low degree
Dared not stop to ask for tea

Timothy Tompkins king of cats
Never dined on mice or rats
Such mundane fare was not his dish
Timothy feasted on meat and fish.

CLOUD PICTURES

Sally and Connie, Dolly and Meg
Lay on the ground with me and with Peg
Laughing and talking in the warm sun
Each telling our stories one by one

Of fairies and elves and princes tall
Dragons and tigers, in the clouds brawl
Wonders we find in the sky above
Fill our hearts with joy, beauty to love

Our hands and legs stretched out toe to toe
On the ground we lay row upon row
Spending our day having so much fun
All laughing and watching what's to come

All red and then brown we do become
The hot summer sun baking us done
Clouds sweeping the sky filling our eyes
All manner of shapes covering the skies

Sally and Connie, Dolly and Meg
Laying all in a row, leg to leg
Watching the clouds making pictures new
Lions and tigers and dragons too

So much fun we all have toe to toe
Without a care and nary a woe
Our cloud pictures and tales fill the air
A game we can play without a care.

An Author's Note

I began this project to bridge the expanse of time between my grandmother and me. From there, it became a passion to share both her writing and mine, with a wider audience. These pages give a glimpse of childhood past, a place of serenity, lightness of spirit, and love.

This is the second edition of Wee Three: A Mother's Love in Verse. It is a place where the hustle and bustle of everyday life can be thrown off and we can return to the pure joy of innocence. Let go of stress and anxiety that today's world brings and restore us to a more carefree time. Hopefully this book will help all who read it, remember the cherished dreams of our youth.

My own childhood was a mixed bag. Growing up in a small town in, Northern Minnesota's mining country, wasn't the ideal life for me. It didn't leave me with the best of memories. Like so many children, life carries its traumas. When I wrote, Wee Three, I had to dig deep inside myself for every scrap of happy memory that I could find. I had to relearn how to look at the world through the innocent eyes of a child.

www.ingramcontent.com/pod-product-compliance
Lightning Source LLC
Chambersburg PA
CBHW070801050426

42452CB00012B/2448